Personal Development

MW01530526

# TABLE OF CONTENTS

*Cover Art by*
Matthew Archambault

**Black & White Illustrations by**
Ken Landgraf

# EDCON
## *Publishing Group*

**Copyright © 2006**
**AV Concepts Corporation**
**Edcon Publishing Group**

**Find More Products Like this at:**
**www.rempub.com**
**1-800-826-4740**

Printed in U.S.A.
ISBN# 1-55576-379-0

# Anger Management

# Anger Management

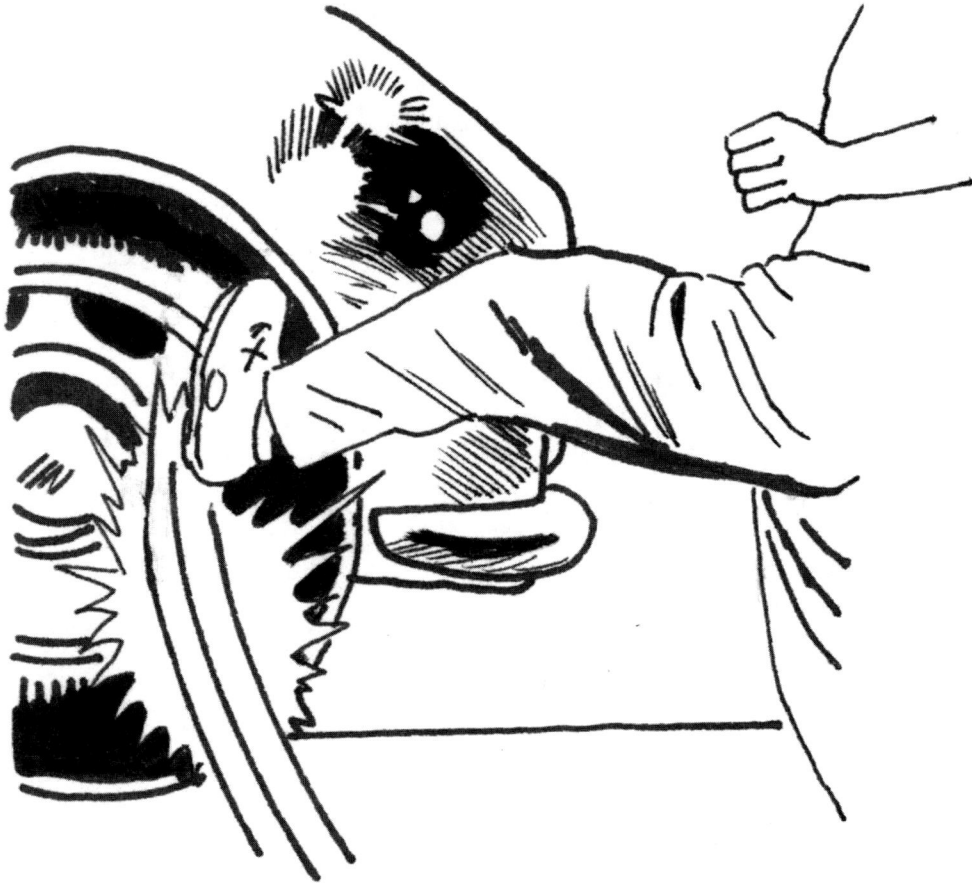

"This dumb car!
It never runs when I want it to!"

Anger. Everybody gets it. It's a natural emotion. It causes your blood pressure to rise, increases your heart rate and breathing, and makes the pupils of your eyes get smaller.

We use heat to describe anger, such as "hot under the collar" or "breathing fire." Sometimes colors are used to describe anger, like "seeing red" or being "purple with rage."

# Anger Management

"Oh, no!"

Anger is a condition that results from being hurt or frustrated. Most of the things that cause anger are EXTERNAL, or outside the body. It is frustration that results in failure to achieve a goal.

"Stupid wagon!"

# Anger Management

An attack on your self-concept or your values can cause you to get angry. We must learn to manage anger by reducing it or re-directing it in an appropriate manner – like a bullfighter directing and controlling the bull's anger.

The first step in anger management is for us to recognize what it is that makes us angry, and then learn to eliminate it. It's important that we don't keep our anger "bottled up" inside of us.

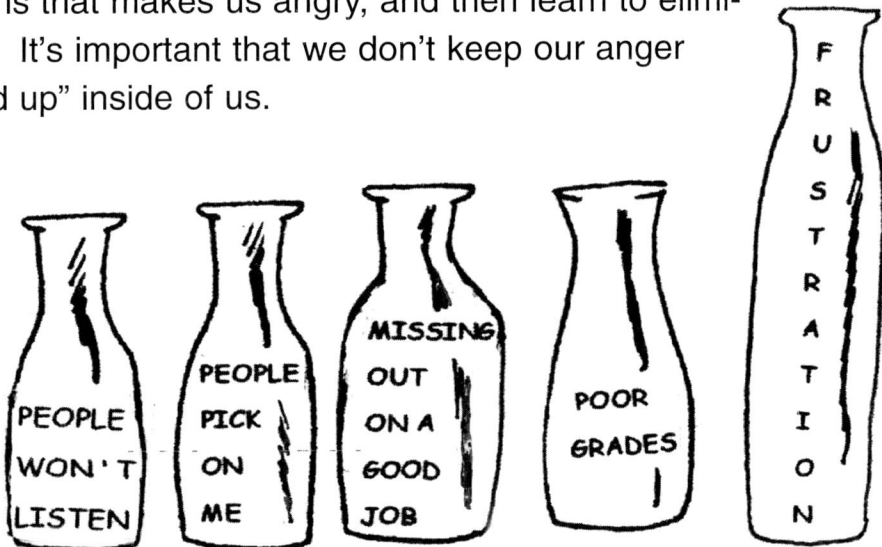

# Anger Management

> 1. **Anxiety**
> 2. **Depression**
> 3. **Self-pity**
> 4. **Apathy**

Anger can be destructive and dangerous. It can result in ANXIETY, DEPRESSION, SELF-PITY, APATHY –

> 1. **Skin rashes**
> 2. **High blood pressure**
> 3. **Ulcers**

and physical conditions like SKIN RASHES, HIGH BLOOD PRESSURE and ULCERS.

Repeatedly being late or absent, losing things, and even vandalism can result from displaced anger. Suicide, murder, and war have been blamed on anger.

By listening to your emotions and learning to read your body signs, you will begin to recognize when you are becoming angry.

When your mouth becomes dry, the palms of your hands become wet, you begin to breathe more quickly, and your body becomes warm, then you could be getting angry. Once you identify the causes of your anger, you can make a graph of each occurrence. This graph will make you aware of your causes of anger.

The following are 5 techniques that can be included in your anger management plan. They are:

> **MENTAL CONDITIONING**
> **RELAXATION STRATEGIES**
> **AVOIDANCE TECHNIQUES**
> **VERBAL RESPONSES**
> **PHYSICAL ACTIVITIES**

# Anger Management

MENTAL CONDITIONING requires you to prepare yourself for an anger response *before* it occurs. It's important to change your pattern of thinking about anger arousal situations. Read how Bill, Nancy, and Mary use self-sentences and mental thinking to prevent their anger.

"This is going to make me angry, but I'm going to deal with it in an intelligent manner," said Bill.

"Why should I let it upset me?" said Nancy. "The sun will rise tomorrow and it will be another day."

Mary said, "I'm getting tense. I better take a couple of deep breaths and relax, slow down, and think about a favorite place. Will it change the world if I don't get my way?"

---

**SELF-SENTENCES
DEEP BREATH RELAXATION
VISUAL IMAGERY**

---

These students used RELAXATION STRATEGIES such as self-sentences, deep breath relaxation, and visual imagery to eliminate their psychological tensions and prevent anger.

Fred knows that when he shoots basketball with Henry and Hal, he always gets angry. So he has decided to stop playing basketball with Henry and Hal and avoid his angry feelings.

If a person always makes you angry, then AVOIDANCE of that person would be one way to reduce your anger.

Dr. Weissinger, a psychologist and author, suggests that if you find yourself in the middle of an argument, you should say, "I'M BEGINNING TO FEEL ANGRY, AND I WANT TO TAKE A TIME-OUT." By stating that you want to take a "time-out," you'll increase your confidence and control in managing angry situations.

# Anger Management

"Shawn, you hurt my feelings when you said I looked dumb. I would prefer that you didn't say that to me."

**VERBAL RESPONSES**

I DON'T SHOUT.

I FEEL GOOD.

HE KNOWS HOW I FEEL.

I WAS ASSERTIVE.

WE'RE STILL FRIENDS.

# Anger Management

Clear and honest communication of anger feelings is the best method of venting our anger or displeasure. At the same time, it establishes boundaries for acceptable communication.

By verbally expressing her feelings about Shawn's comments, Nancy did not bottle up her anger. At the same time, she attempted to change Shawn's behavior and prevent future anger.

Speaking assertively at the time of the incident will also give her a good feeling about her actions and her friendship with Shawn.

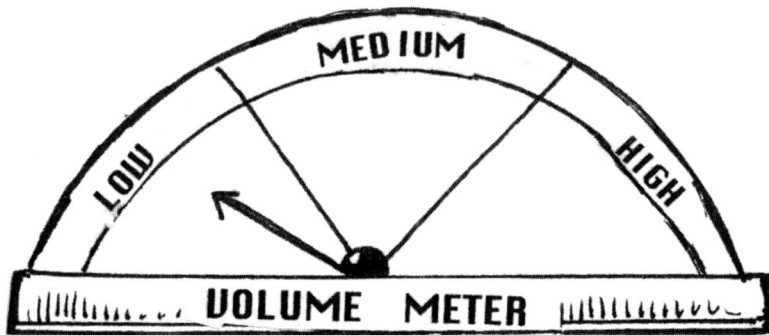

When Nancy spoke, she controlled her volume. She did not shout or raise her voice because she knew that when you shout at someone, it makes them want to shout back – and then you're in a shouting match. When you are angry, always use your softest voice.

```
OPENNESS
+
HONESTY
= FRIENDSHIP
```

# Anger Management

## COMMUNICATE  YOUR FEELINGS

Learn to communicate your feelings in an honest and open manner that is sincere, but not offensive.  Speak assertively in a calm, soft voice.

## USE ANGER MANAGEMENT TECHNIQUES

Use your anger management techniques either individually, or in combination, recording and evaluating the effectiveness of each technique.

## USE THE INSTANT REPLAY GAME

Use the instant replay game to discover how you handled an angry situation.  Think about both your verbal and physical responses.  Could you have used other techniques?

Anger is an emotion.  All of us get angry.  Sometimes anger is caused by a misunderstanding caused by faulty thinking or improper interpretations of the actions of others.  It is often directed at a close friend or someone we like very much.

By discovering what makes you angry and assuming responsibility for improving your angry feelings, you will become healthy, happy, and relaxed.  And you'll have lots of close friends!

# Anger Management

*TRUE (T) or FALSE (F)*

_____ 1.  Anger is not a natural emotion.  Intelligent people never get angry.

_____ 2.  When we become angry, there is a physical change in our breathing and heart rate.

_____ 3.  Anger is often caused by a frustration in not achieving a goal.

_____ 4.  Self-awareness is the first step to managing our anger.

_____ 5.  Young children are not able to express their anger.

_____ 6.  Most mature adults express their anger verbally, rather than physically.

_____ 7.  It is important to identify the source of our anger.

_____ 8.  Displaced anger is focused directly on what has made us angry.

_____ 9.  Anger cannot really harm us, so we should not become too concerned about it.

_____ 10. If your mouth becomes dry and the palms of your hands become wet, you may be getting angry.

*Answer Key is found on page 48.*

# Anger Management

*MATCHING*

Match the anger management technique in Column A to its example in Column B.

### COLUMN A

_____ 1. Mental Conditioning

_____ 2. Relaxation Strategy

_____ 3. Avoidance Technique

_____ 4. Verbal Response

_____ 5. Physical Activity

### COLUMN B

A. A game of baseball

B. "Please don't say that to me."

C. Close your eyes and breathe deeply

D. "Me worry! The sun will rise tomorrow."

E. "So long. I'm going to Mike's house."

*Answer Key is found on page 48.*

Following are five emotions.  Write a short sentence describing the last time YOU experienced the emotion and your resulting behavior, actions, or feelings.

EMOTION: **JOY**;  LAST EXPERIENCE:


BEHAVIOR OR FEELINGS:


EMOTION: **LOVE**;  LAST EXPERIENCE:


BEHAVIOR OR FEELINGS:


EMOTION: **FEAR**;  LAST EXPERIENCE:


BEHAVIOR OR FEELINGS:


EMOTION: **ANGER**;  LAST EXPERIENCE:


BEHAVIOR OR FEELINGS:


EMOTION: **GRIEF**;  LAST EXPERIENCE:


BEHAVIOR OR FEELINGS

# Don't Bug Me!

## RULES OF THE GAME
### 1. Choose the right time to talk.

The first rule is simple. Always approach adults when they can listen to what you have to say without interruption. Let's return to Jackie and her father.

"Is the game over, Dad?"

"Yeah. We won 17-13. Whew! What a game. Now, what were you saying you needed?"

The second rule of the game is a little trickier. Let's look at the problem Peter and his dad are having.

"Dad, I'm glad you're home. I need your help with my science project. Can you come and look at it right now?"

"Pete, everybody at work today had a problem for me to fix. Machines didn't work – deliveries didn't show up – and one employee quit. I've had it!"

# Don't Bug Me!

"But, Dad, I thought you were interested in my project."

"Well, of course I am, Pete, but I'm beat and just can't do it tonight.  Now, don't bug me!"

೪೦  ೪೨

Sometimes, adults just need to be understood.

---

### RULES OF THE GAME

1.  Choose the right time to talk.
2.  **Use reflective listening.**

---

The second rule of the game is to use reflective listening.  By reflecting back someone's feelings, we let them know that we understand where they are coming from.
Let's see how it works for Pete.

"I guess you had a hard day all right," said Pete.  "You must be exhausted.  I'll keep my music down until you've had a chance to rest."

"Thanks for understanding, Pete.  Uh, wake me up in a little bit.  I'd like to see how your project is coming."

೪೦  ೪೨

# Don't Bug Me!

As you have just read, both agreeing with the other person and softening your voice can de-escalate conflict and improve the communication process.

---

### RULES OF THE GAME

1. Choose the right time to talk.
2. Use reflective listening.
3. "I" message
4. Agree with the other person when you can.
5. Soften your voice.
6. **Negotiate a trade.**

---

The sixth rule is a combination of the others, or what might be called, "negotiating a trade." Let's look at the following situation and see if we can help resolve it.

"Bob, I want you to clean your room this morning before you leave."

Bob moaned. "Mom, I told the guys I'd be at school early this morning so we could work out some plays."

"We're having company, and you'll clean your room today," said Bob's mom, pointing a finger, "whether you play football or not. Is that clear?"

"But, Mom, I've got to play a big game this afternoon," cried Bob.

# Don't Bug Me!

In this case, both Mom and Bob are losing. The sixth rule may be the solution to their problem – negotiate a trade.

To negotiate a trade, first find out what is important to each person.

> ## TRY TO MAKE A PLAN THAT LETS BOTH PEOPLE WIN!

Let's read how it works.

Bob asked his mother, "Why is it so important that I clean my room today? We've had company before, and you just shut my door."

"The people who are coming are very dear and old friends. They're your godparents. They haven't seen you since you were a baby. They're looking forward to seeing you. And I'm sure they'll want to see your room, too."

"Oh, I see," said Bob. "Well, I guess I could get everything picked up this morning, if that would help. And Mom, if you could just vacuum and dust my room, I could help you with something as a trade."

"Okay, Bob. I think that's a good plan," said Bob's mom, smiling. "I'd be happy to have you rake the leaves and help in the kitchen tomorrow."

# Don't Bug Me!

Not every rule that we've read about will work in every situation. You have to practice and find out what works for YOU.
Now, let's review the rules.

---

### RULES OF THE GAME

1. Choose the right time to talk.

2. Use reflective listening.

3. Use an "I" message.

4. Agree with the other person when you can.

5. Soften your voice.

6. Negotiate a trade.

---

Follow these rules and you'll never hear someone say, "Don't bug me!"

# Don't Bug Me!

## FILL IN THE BLANKS

Fill in the blank in each sentence with the correct word(s) from the box below.

| | |
|---|---|
| "I" message | agree |
| listen | lower your voice |
| reflective listening | negotiate a trade |

1. Always approach adults when they can _____ to what you have to say.

2. By using _____ _____, we let people know that we understand their feelings.

3. If you have a problem and tell the other person how you feel, then you would be using the _____ technique.

4. Sometimes the best way to begin to effectively communicate with someone is to _____ with them.

5. Your communication skills are sure to improve if you don't accuse someone of doing something and you remember to _____ _____ _____ when talking.

6. If you can _____ _____ _____, you can often avoid a conflict.

Answers can be found on page 48.

# Answer Key

## ANGER MANAGEMENT

### TRUE OR FALSE

1. F
2. T
3. T
4. T
w
6. T
7. F
8. F
9. F
10. T

### MATCHING

1. D
2. C
3. E
4. B
5. A

## DON'T BUG ME!

### FILL IN THE BLANKS

1. listen
2. reflective listening
3. "I" message
4. agree
5. lower your voice
6. negotiate a trade

## STICKING UP FOR NUMBER ONE

### FILL IN THE BLANKS

1. fear / insecurity
2. recognize
3. time
4. long-term
5. in charge
6. fear rejection
7. values
8. decision making
9. more successful